D0326972

PANTHEON BO

AUS

I

A SURVIVOR'S TALE

MY FATHER
BLEEDS
HISTORY

art spiegelman

OKS NEW YORK

"The Jews are undoubtedly a race,
but they are not human."
Adolf Hitler

Thanks to Ken and Flo Jacobs, Ernie Gehr, Paul Pavel, Louise Fili, and Steven Heller,
whose appreciation and moral support have helped this book find its shape.

Thanks to Mala Spiegelman for her help in translating Polish books and documents,
and for wanting *Maus* to happen.

And thanks to Françoise Mouly for her intelligence and integrity,
for her editorial skills, and for her love.

Copyright © 1973, 1980, 1981, 1982, 1983, 1984, 1985, 1986 by Art Spiegelman.

All rights reserved under International and Pan-American Copyright Conventions.
Published in the United States by Pantheon Books, a division of Random House, Inc.,
New York, and simultaneously in Canada by Random House of Canada Limited, Toronto.

Chapters 1 through 6 first appeared, in somewhat different form, in *Raw* magazine between 1980 and 1985.

"Prisoner on the Hell Planet" originally appeared in *Short Order Comix #1,* 1973

Library of Congress Cataloging-in-Publication Data
Spiegelman, Art.
Maus: a survivor's tale.
I: My Father Bleeds History
1. Spiegelman, Vladek — Comic books, strips, etc.
2. Holocaust, Jewish (1939-1945) — Poland — Biography Comic books, strips, etc.
3. Holocaust survivors — United States — Biography — Comic books, strips, etc.
4. Spiegelman, Art — Comic books, strips, etc.
5. Children of the Holocaust survivors — United States — Biography — Comic books, strips, etc.
I. Title.
D810.J4S643   1986   940.53'15'03924024   86-42642
ISBN 394-54155-3 (hardcover); 679-73974-2 (paperback)

For more information about *Raw* magazine, write to Raw Books and Graphics,
27 Greene Street, New York, New York 10013.

Manufactured in U.S.A.
9876543

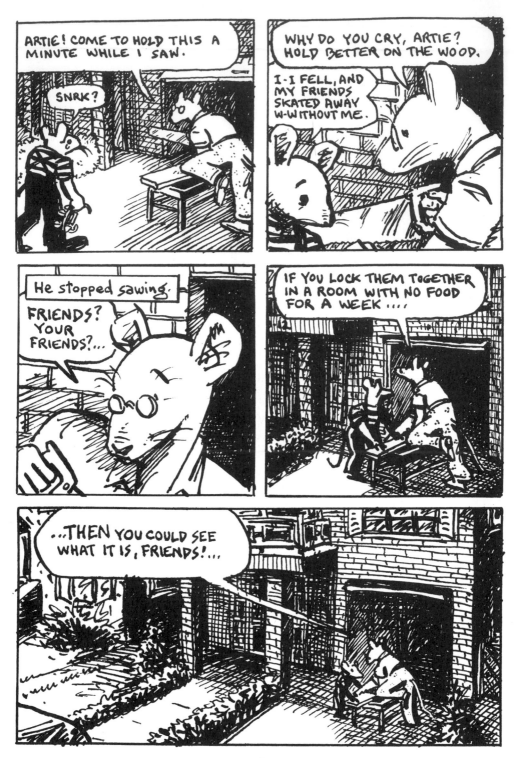

6

MY FATHER BLEEDS HISTORY

(MID-1930s TO WINTER 1944)

CONTENTS

FOR ANJA

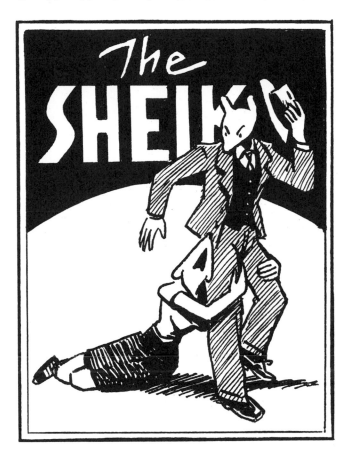

I went out to see my Father in Rego Park. I hadn't seen him in a long time- we weren't that close.

POPPA!

OI, ARTIE. YOU'RE LATE. I WAS WORRIED.

IT'S A SHAME FRANÇOISE ALSO DIDN'T COME.

UH-HUH. SHE SENDS REGARDS.

He had aged a lot since I saw him last. My Mother's suicide and his two heart attacks had taken their toll.

MALA! LOOK WHO'S HERE! ARTIE!

He was remarried. Mala knew my parents in Poland before the war.

She was a survivor too, like most of my parents' friends.

HI, ARTIE. LET ME TAKE YOUR COAT.

THE DINNER IS ON THE TABLE.

ACCH, MALA!

A WIRE HANGER YOU GIVE HIM! I HAVEN'T SEEN ARTIE IN ALMOST TWO YEARS- WE HAVE PLENTY WOODEN HANGERS.

They didn't get along.

After dinner he took me into my old room...

COME—WE'LL TALK WHILE I PEDAL...

IT'S GOOD FOR MY HEART, THE PEDALING. BUT, TELL ME, HOW IS IT BY YOU? HOW IS GOING THE COMICS BUSINESS?

I STILL WANT TO DRAW THAT BOOK ABOUT YOU...

THE ONE I USED TO TALK TO YOU ABOUT..

ABOUT YOUR LIFE IN POLAND, AND THE WAR.

IT WOULD TAKE **MANY** BOOKS, MY LIFE, AND NO ONE WANTS ANYWAY TO HEAR SUCH STORIES.

I WANT TO HEAR IT. START WITH MOM... TELL ME HOW YOU MET.

BETTER YOU SHOULD SPEND YOUR TIME TO MAKE DRAWINGS WHAT WILL BRING YOU SOME MONEY...

BUT, IF YOU WANT, I CAN TELL YOU...I LIVED THEN IN CZESTOCHOWA, A SMALL CITY NOT FAR FROM THE BORDER OF GERMANY...

I WAS IN TEXTILES—BUY-ING AND SELLING—I DIDN'T MAKE MUCH, BUT ALWAYS I COULD MAKE A LIVING.

13

14

15

THE NEXT MORNING WE ALL MET TOGETHER. MY COUSIN AND ANJA SPOKE SOMETIMES IN ENGLISH.

HOW YOU LIKE HIM?

HE'S A HANDSOME BOY AND SEEMS VERY NICE.

THEY COULDN'T KNOW I UNDERSTOOD.

WELL—I PROMISED TO BE HOME EARLY... I'LL LEAVE YOU TWO ALONE

YOU KNOW, YOU SHOULD BE CAREFUL SPEAKING ENGLISH— A "STRANGER" COULD UNDERSTAND.

Y-YOU KNOW ENGLISH?

DID YOU STUDY IT IN SCHOOL?

I HAD TO QUIT SCHOOL AT ABOUT 14 TO WORK.

...BUT I TOOK PRIVATE LESSONS... I ALWAYS DREAMED OF GOING TO AMERICA.

IT'S A SHAME YOU HAVE TO RETURN TO CZESTOCHOWA SO SOON.

YES—BUT I HAVE MY BUSINESS.

HAVE YOU A PHONE AT HOME?

AS SOON I CAME BACK TO CZESTOCHOWA, SHE CALLED — ONCE A DAY...TWICE... EVERY DAY WE TALKED.

16

17

MOM WASN'T THAT ATTRACTIVE, HUH?

NOT SO LIKE LUCIA... BUT IF YOU TALKED A LITTLE TO HER, YOU STARTED LOVING HER MORE AND MORE.

ONE TIME WE WALKED INTO THE DIRECTOR FROM HER SCHOOL...

YOU'RE VERY LUCKY, MR. SPIEGELMAN...

...YOU DON'T KNOW WHAT A GIRL YOU'RE GETTING—I'VE HAD MANY STUDENTS...

...BUT NEVER ONE AS SENSITIVE AND INTELLIGENT AS ANNA!

YES—THAT'S WHY I PICKED HER.

I WISH YOU COULD VISIT ME IN CZESTOCHOWA—I'D LIKE TO SHOW YOU OFF TO MY FRIENDS.

I'VE BEGGED MY MOTHER TO LET ME GO—BUT SHE'S SO RELIGIOUS AND OLD-FASHIONED.

...SHE WOULD NEVER ALLOW ME TO GO TO A BACHELOR'S APARTMENT!

ANJA'S PARENTS WERE ANXIOUS SHE SHOULD BE MARRIED. SHE WAS 24; I WAS THEN 30.

OH, MY PARENTS WOULD LIKE YOU TO COME TO DINNER TOMORROW NIGHT.

THE ZYLBERBERG FAMILY WAS VERY WELL OFF—MILLIONAIRES!

ACH! HERE I FORGOT TO TELL SOMETHING FROM *BEFORE* I MOVED TO SOSNOWIEC BUT AFTER OUR ENGAGEMENT WAS MADE.

ONE EVENING THE BELL RANG ...

LUCIA

WHAT ARE YOU DOING HERE? I'M ON MY WAY OUT.

I-I'LL COME WITH YOU.

NO, YOU CAN'T COME WI—

PLEASE, VLADEK!

SHE FELL ON THE FLOOR AND HELD STRONG MY LEGS.

DON'T RUN AWAY!

I SAW NOW THAT I WENT TOO FAR WITH HER.

SLAM!

I RAN OUT TO MY FRIEND WHAT INTRO-DUCED US. HE WENT TO CALM HER DOWN AND TOOK HER HOME.

25

For the next few months I went back to visit my father quite regularly, to hear his story.

ABOUT MOM...

...11...12...13...

—UH... WHAT ARE YOU DOING, POP?

I'M MAKING INTO DAILY PORTIONS MY PILLS. ...14...15...

...16...17...18...

SO MANY?

IT'S 6 PILLS FOR THE HEART, 1 FOR DIABETES... AND MAYBE 25 OR 30 VITAMINS.

FOR MY CONDITION I MUST FIGHT TO SAVE MYSELF. DOCTORS, THEY ONLY GIVE ME "JUNK FOOD"...

..THAT'S HOW I CALL PRESCRIPTION DRUGS NOW. I STUDY THIS IN MY PREVENTION MAGAZINES... MAYBE YOU WANT TO READ?

NO THANKS.

ABOUT MOM — DID SHE HAVE ANY BOYFRIENDS BEFORE SHE MET YOU?

NOT ROMANTIC... BUT ONE TALL BOY FROM WARSAW

HE WAS... A COMMUNIST!

28

WHEN I FOUND OUT THIS STORY, I WAS READY TO BREAK THE MARRIAGE.

I TOLD HER "ANJA, IF YOU WANT ME YOU HAVE TO GO MY WAY...

IF YOU WANT YOUR COMMUNIST FRIENDS, THEN I CAN'T STAY IN THIS HOUSE!"

AND SHE WAS A GOOD GIRL, AND OF COURSE SHE STOPPED ALL SUCH THINGS.

WHAT HAPPENED TO THE SEAMSTRESS?

MISS STEFANSKA SAT IN PRISON FOR A LONGER TIME - MAYBE 3 MONTHS.

IT WASN'T ENOUGH EVIDENCE AND FINALLY THE POLICE LEFT HER GO.

FATHER-IN-LAW PAID THE COST FROM THE LAWYERS AND GAVE TO HER SOME MONEY-IT COST MAYBE 15,000 ZLOTYS.

THAT'S A LOT, HUH?

JA, BUT NOT ONLY THIS. AT THE SAME TIME HE DID FOR US EVEN MORE...

YOU KNOW, VLADEK, WHEN YOU AND ANJA GIVE ME A GRANDCHILD, I WANT HIM TO BE WELL-OFF.

WELL, I ALMOST HAVE ENOUGH FROM MY SALES TRIPS TO START UP A TEXTILE SHOP...

A SHOP? PFUI! YOU OUGHT TO HAVE A TEXTILE FACTORY!

THAT WOULD COST A FORTUNE!!

PLEASE - I CAN GIVE YOU THE MONEY AND PLENTY OF CREDIT.

I STARTED A FACTORY IN BIELSKO, AND VISITED TO ANJA EVERY WEEK-END.

33

34

IN THE EVENINGS WE WENT EITHER TO THE THEATER OR TO DANCE IN THE CAFE.

DID I TELL YOU THE TRAGEDY ABOUT THE PILLOW MY FAMILY LOST AT THE START OF THE 1914 WAR! I WAS SEVEN.... WE LIVED TOO CLOSE TO THE BORDER .... IT WASN'T SAFE...

I TOLD HER MANY JOKES AND STORIES TO KEEP HER BUSY...

...SO WE TOOK WHAT WE COULD ON A WAGON PULLED BY FOUR HORSES AND WENT TO MY GRANDFATHER'S HOME IN RADOMSKO.

SOMEONE RODE PAST US AND TOLD US THAT WE'D DROPPED A PILLOW A FEW MILES BACK. A GUY TRAVELING TO AMSTOW PICKED IT UP.

IMAGINE - MY FATHER NEVER RODE A HORSE BEFORE .... BUT HE UNHITCHED ONE FROM THE WAGON AND RODE TOWARD AMSTOW..

WE WAITED AND WAITED.. MOTHER STARTED CRYING: "SURELY HE FELL AND GOT KILLED!" SHE HAD BEGGED HIM TO "LET THE PILLOW GO AND TAKE ALL OUR TROUBLES WITH IT!"

THE HORSE WAS BONY AND DIDN'T HAVE A SADDLE... FINALLY, LATE THAT NIGHT, FATHER RODE BACK WITH THE PILLOW ...UNDER HIS BLOODY "TUCHUS"...

SO, FATHER GOT HIS PILLOW BACK ...BUT HE COULDN'T SIT DOWN FOR THE REST OF THE WAR!

I LOVE YOU, VLADEK.

AND SHE WAS SO LAUGHING AND SO HAPPY, SO HAPPY, THAT SHE APPROACHED EACH TIME AND KISSED ME, SO HAPPY SHE WAS.

35

WE STAYED MAYBE 3 MONTHS, AND WHEN WE CAME BACK, ANJA WAS COMPLETELY DIFFERENT FROM WHEN SHE LEFT.

YOO HOO, POPPA!

ANJA! YOU LOOK LIKE A MILLION!

LISTEN, VLADEK.... I DIDN'T WANT YOU TO WORRY WHILE YOU WERE AT THE SANITARIUM, BUT —

—BRACE YOURSELF—THE BIELSKO FACTORY HAS BEEN **ROBBED**!

WHAT!

IT HAPPENED LAST MONTH. THEY TOOK **EVERYTHING**!

AI! AI! AI!

I DIDN'T EVEN HAVE TIME TO INSURE IT BEFORE WE LEFT.

WELL, AT LEAST I CAN HELP YOU BUILD IT UP AGAIN.

WERE YOU LOOTED AS PART OF SOME KIND OF ANTI-SEMITIC ACTIVITY?

I DON'T **THINK** THIS WAS IT. JUST A ROBBERY...

...LIKE WHEN THEY ROBBED US IN REGO PARK HERE, LAST YEAR.

WELL.... IN BIELSKO, FATHER-IN-LAW HELPED US AGAIN TO ESTABLISH OURSELVES...

IN A COUPLE MONTHS WE WERE WELL-OFF— QUITE WELL-OFF... A WORKING FACTORY, A 2 BEDROOM APARTMENT, A POLISH GOVERNESS, AND EVEN A MAID.

LOOK, RICHIEU, POPPA'S HOME!

YOU LOOK UPSET, VLADEK.

THERE WAS ANOTHER RIOT DOWNTOWN TODAY.

...EVERYONE YELLING, "JEWS OUT! JEWS OUT!"...EVEN TWO PEOPLE KILLED. THE POLICE JUST WATCHED!

IT'S THOSE NAZIS STIRRING EVERYBODY UP!

WHEN IT COMES TO JEWS, THE POLES DON'T NEED MUCH STIRRING UP!

MRS. SPIEGELMAN— HOW CAN YOU SAY SUCH A THING. I THINK OF YOU AS PART OF MY OWN FAMILY!

I'M SORRY, JANINA. I DIDN'T MEAN YOU! I'M JUST WORRIED!

MAYBE WE SHOULD MOVE AWAY, LIKE SOME OTHERS HAVE.

IF THINGS GET REALLY BAD WE'LL RUN BACK TO SOSNOWIEC.

WHY WOULD SOSNOWIEC BE ANY SAFER THAN BIELSKO?

WE THOUGHT THEN, THAT HITLER WANTED ONLY THE PARTS FROM POLAND, LIKE BIELSKO, WHAT USED TO BE PARTS FROM GERMANY BEFORE THE FIRST WORLD WAR.

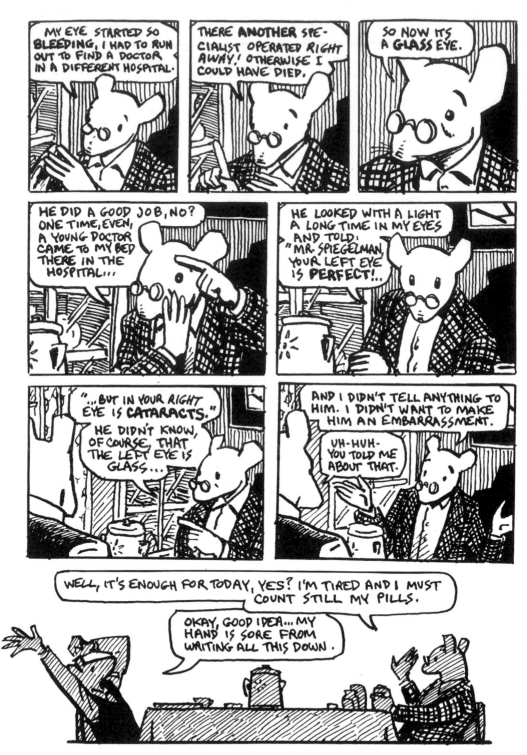

40

I visited my father more often in order to get more information about his past..

43

44

47

THEN BULLETS CAME IN MY DIRECTION.

PNNNG

I DUG *DEEPER* MY TRENCH BUT I STOPPED TO SHOOT.

WHY SHOULD I KILL ANYONE?

PWNNG

BUT WHEN I LOOKED IN MY GUN, I SAW... A TREE! !!!!

AND THE TREE WAS ACTUALLY MOVING!

I MUST BE SEEING THINGS. HOW CAN A TREE RUN?

WELL, IF IT MOVED, I HAD TO SHOOT!

AKH!

PNG

IT HELD UP A HAND TO SHOW IT WAS HURT. TO SURRENDER.

BUT I KEPT SHOOTING AND SHOOTING. UNTIL FINALLY THE TREE STOPPED MOVING. WHO KNOWS; OTHERWISE HE COULD HAVE SHOT ME!

48

51

SO WE LIVED AND WORKED A FEW WEEKS IN THE STABLE UNTIL THEY TOOK US TO AN EVEN *BIGGER* PRISONER OF WAR CAMP.

BRRR. THE POLISH PRISONERS GET **HEATED** CABINS.

YES, AND WE'RE JUST LEFT TO FREEZE IN THESE TENTS.

IT WAS TERRIBLE COLD THAT AUTUMN. ALL OVER EUROPE IT WAS SO FREEZING THAT BIRDS FELL FROM TREES.

TO KEEP WARM WE HAD ONLY OUR SUMMER UNIFORMS AND A THIN BLANKET.

AT LEAST IF THEY GAVE US ENOUGH TO EAT.

THE OTHER PRISONERS GET **TWO** MEALS A DAY. WE JEWS GET ONLY A CRUST OF BREAD AND A LITTLE SOUP.

GOOD MORNING, VLADEK.

WHERE ARE YOU GOING?

TO BATHE IN THE RIVER.

YOU'VE GONE CRAZY.

BRRR I'LL BE **CLEAN**! AND I'LL FEEL WARM ALL DAY BY COMPARISON.

MANY OTHERS GOT FROSTBITE WOUNDS. IN THE WOUNDS WAS PUS, AND IN THE PUS WAS LICE.

WHEN MY COMRADES SAW I WAS GOING, THEY TOO REGISTERED.

WE WERE RIGHT AWAY SENT TO A BIG GERMAN COMPANY.

WE WERE TAKEN TO NICE WOODEN HOUSES. WE GOT SOUP AND WE GOT BREAD...

LOOK! A STOVE!

AND REAL BEDS!

WITH SHEETS AND PILLOWS!

AND FOR A WHOLE DAY WE ONLY RESTED AND GOT BACK OUR STRENGTH.

AH- IT SEEMS LIKE YEARS SINCE I'VE FELT WARM OR BEEN IN A BED!

YES- FUNNY, ISN'T IT? IT'S ONLY A LITTLE OVER 2 MONTHS SINCE WE WERE DRAFTED.

I'M WORRIED THOUGH, VLADEK- WHO KNOWS WHAT KIND OF WORK THEY'LL GIVE US.

IT DOESN'T MATTER..

..ANYTHING IS BETTER THAN ROTTING IN THOSE TENTS.

I SUPPOSE.

THE NEXT DAY WE WERE GIVEN SHOVELS AND PICKS ...

...THINGS WHAT WE NEVER HELD IN OUR HANDS BEFORE.

AND THE WORK WAS REALLY VERY HARD— WE HAD TO MOVE MOUNTAINS.

MOUNTAIN

VALLEY

THE HILLS WERE MAYBE 3 OR 4 YARDS HIGH. WE HAD TO MAKE IT LEVEL.

SOME COMPLAINED —THOSE WHAT WERE TOO OLD OR WEAK FOR SUCH WORK:

I—I CAN'T TAKE ANYMORE.

WORTHLESS JEW!

IF YOU'RE UNHAPPY—GO BACK TO THE P.O.W. CAMP.

IT'S OKAY—WE'LL HELP YOU WHEN NO ONE IS LOOKING.

WE TRIED TO HELP, BUT—WHAT YOU THINK?—SOME WENT BACK TO THE TENTS TO FREEZE AND TO STARVE.

BUT WHAT HAP- PENED TO THEM, I DON'T KNOW.

STILL, EIGHTY PER CENT STAYED. THERE WAS ENOUGH TO EAT, AND A WARM BED. IT WAS BETTER TO STAY...

...ALWAYS I WENT TO SLEEP EXHAUSTED. AND ONE NIGHT I HAD A DREAM...

"DON'T WORRY..."

A VOICE WAS TALKING TO ME. IT WAS, I THINK, MY DEAD GRANDFATHER...

"...DON'T WORRY, MY CHILD..."

IT WAS SO REAL, THIS VOICE...

"YOU WILL COME OUT OF THIS PLACE - FREE! ...ON THE DAY OF PARSHAS TRUMA."

I WOKE UP RIGHT AWAY. AND WHEN I WENT TO SLEEP, AGAIN IT WAS: "PARSHAS TRUMA! PARSHAS TRUMA!"

SO WHAT'S PARSHAS TRUMA?

EACH WEEK, ON SATURDAY, WE READ A SECTION FROM THE TORAH.

THIS IS SO CALLED - A PARSHA... AND ONE WEEK EACH YEAR IT IS PARSHAS TRUMA.

BEFORE WORK A FEW FROM US PRAYED. IT WAS A RABBI THERE WITH US.

ONE MOMENT, RABBI. WHEN WILL WE READ PARSHAS TRUMA?

PARSHAS TRUMA?...

...IN THE MIDDLE OF FEBRUARY—ALMOST THREE MONTHS FROM NOW. WHY?

THREE MONTHS—AND EVERY DAY WAS FOR US A YEAR!

I TOLD HIM MY DREAM...

LET'S HOPE IT'S TRUE. I'M AFRAID WE'LL NEVER GET OUT OF HERE.

DURING THE JOURNEY I SAT WITH THE RABBI.

SO, MY SON. NOW I SEE YOU ARE A "ROH-EH HANOLED," ONE WHO SEES WHAT THE FUTURE WILL BRING.

HEY! THIS TRAIN SEEMS TO BE *PASSING* SOSNOWIEC!

WHEN THEY DIDN'T STOP THE TRAIN I BECAME VERY WORRIED.

YOU SEE, THE NAZIS DIVIDED POLAND INTO PIECES: PROTECTORATE AND REICH, WITH A GUARDED BORDER BETWEEN.

THE TRAIN WENT COMPLETELY *PAST* MY PART OF POLAND—THE REICH—AND STOPPED ONLY IN THE PROTECTORATE.

THOSE WITH PAPERS FOR KRAKOW—OUT!

BALTIC SEA
LITHUANIA
E. PRUSSIA
(annexed to Russia)
P O L A N D
SOVIET UNION
GERMANY
WARSAW
LUBLIN
SOSNOWIEC
KRAKOW
HUNGARY
SLOVAKIA
RUMANIA

☐ REICH: Annexed to Germany.
☐ PROTECTORATE: German controlled Government.

AND, WHEN IT STOPPED IN WARSAW, THE RABBI GOT OUT.

I'LL WRITE TO YOU.

BUT I NEVER HEARD AGAIN FROM HIM. IT CAME SUCH A MISERY IN WARSAW, ALMOST NONE SURVIVED.

AND THE TRAIN WAS A LONG WAY PAST SOSNOWIEC. THEY TOOK ME UP, UP, VERY FAR—MAYBE 300 MILES—UNTIL WE CAME TO LUBLIN. THERE THEY UNLOADED ALL OF US FROM THE REICH.

IN LUBLIN, THEY TOOK US TO BIG TENTS...

AND THERE WE SAT.

EVENTUALLY CAME SOME PEOPLE TO SEE US FROM THE JEWISH AUTHORITIES...

WHY ARE WE BEING KEPT HERE?

IT'S A VERY BAD SITUA- TION... JUST BEFORE YOU ARRIVED, THERE WAS ANOTHER GROUP OF RE- LEASED WAR PRISONERS...

...TWO DAYS AGO THE NAZIS MARCHED THEM TO A FOREST,...

...AND THEY SHOT ALL OF THEM—THEY KILLED 600 PEOPLE!

WE WERE THE NEXT PARTY!

I THOUGHT YOU WERE RELEASED AS A PRISONER OF WAR!

EXACTLY SO..

INTERNATIONAL LAWS PROTECTED US A LITTLE AS POLISH WAR PRISONERS. BUT A JEW OF THE REICH, ANY- ONE COULD KILL IN THE STREETS!

61

THEN, AS SOON AS IT WAS LIGHT...

SPIEGELMAN!.. SPIEGELMAN!..

VLADEK!

ORBACH! AM I GLAD TO SEE YOU!

AND IN TEN MINUTES, I WAS FREE!

ORBACH WAS A FRIEND FROM MY UNCLE—HE HAD TWO BEAUTIFUL DAUGHTERS NEAR TO MY AGE.

I'M SORRY WE CAN'T OFFER YOU A BETTER MEAL, VLADEK—BUT THE JEWS OF LUBLIN GET VERY FEW FOOD COUPONS.

ONE MOMENT, GIRLS—I HAVE A GIFT FOR EACH OF YOU....

OH MY GOD! CHOCOLATE!

THESE I SAVED FROM A RED CROSS PACKAGE. ALWAYS I SAVED... JUST IN CASE!

EVENTUALLY, WHEN I CAME AGAIN TO SOSNO-WIEC, WE SENT THEM FOOD PACKAGES...

... WE WERE FOR A WHILE A LITTLE BETTER OFF.... AND THEY WROTE BACK VERY HAPPY HOW IT HELPED SURVIVE THEM....

...THEN THEY WROTE THAT THE GERMANS WERE KEEPING THE PACKAGES, AND THEN THEY STOPPED TO WRITE. FINISHED.

WITH ORBACHS' I STAYED A FEW DAYS RECUPERATING. BUT I WAS RESTLESS. HOW COULD I MANAGE TO SNEAK ACROSS THE BORDER TO MY FAMILY?

TRAINS WERE STILL GOING FROM PROTECTORATE TO REICH. ONLY, ONE NEEDED LEGAL PAPERS. OF COURSE, THIS I DIDN'T HAVE ...

...BUT ANYWAY I GOT ON THE TRAIN IN THE DIRECTION I WANTED.

I APPROACHED TO THE TRAIN MAN, A POLE...

MAY I TALK TO YOU FOR A MOMENT?

SURE, SOLDIER.

I STILL HAD ON MY ARMY UNIFORM, AND I DIDN'T LET *KNOW* I WAS A JEW.

YOU'RE A POLE LIKE ME, SO I CAN TRUST YOU...THE STINKING NAZIS HAD ME IN A WAR PRISON...I JUST ESCAPED.

THE POLES WERE VERY BITTER ON THE GERMANS, SO IT WAS GOOD TO SPEAK BAD OF THEM.

I'M TRYING TO GET TO SOSNOWIEC — BACK TO MY FAMILY.

DON'T WORRY... WHEN WE GET TO THE BORDER, HIDE IN HERE.

AND SO THE TRAIN MAN HELPED ME COME BACK TO MY SIDE OF POLAND.

I WALKED FIRST OVER TO MY PARENTS' HOUSE...

...WHAT I THOUGHT I MIGHT NEVER SEE AGAIN.

OY GEVALT! IT'S **VLADEK!**

65

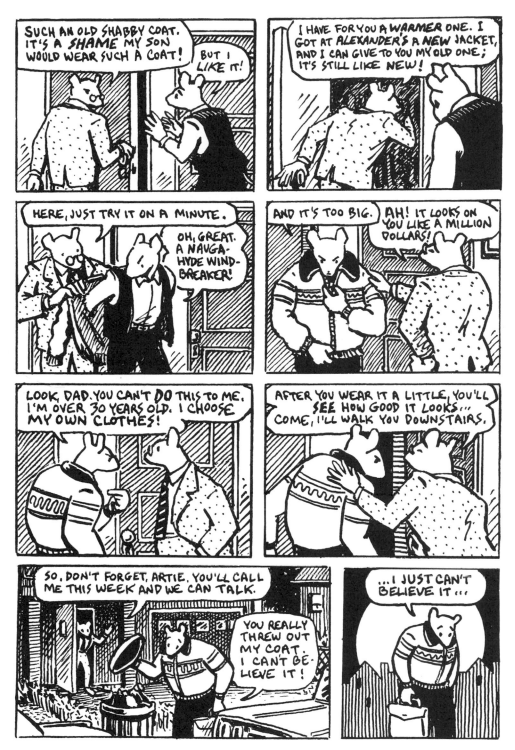

73

74

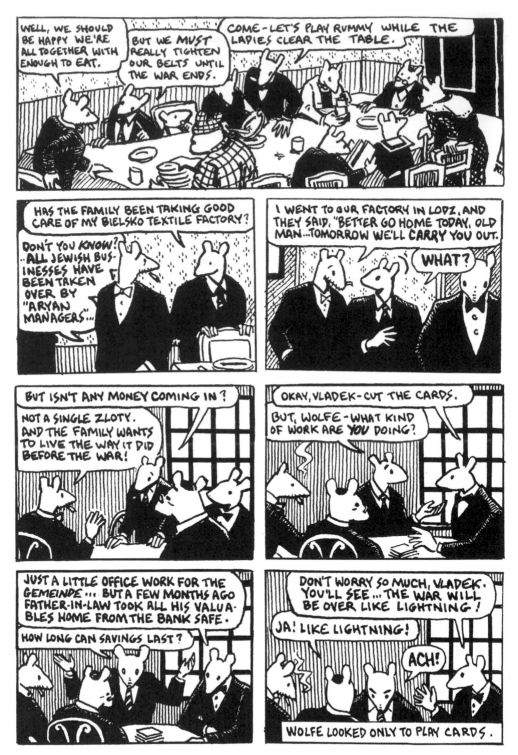

AND SO WE LIVED FOR MORE THAN A YEAR. BUT ALWAYS THINGS CAME A LITTLE WORSE, A LITTLE WORSE...

FATHER-IN-LAW HAD A NICE NEW BEDROOM SET...

THE GERMANS LOOKED TO GRAB SUCH FURNITURE, BECAUSE IN STORES IT WASN'T ANYMORE TO GET.

WOLFE AND I SHLEPPED EVERYTHING VALUABLE DOWNSTAIRS FOR A POLISH NEIGHBOR TO HIDE.

OOF. ARE WE LEAVING THE OTHER BED UPSTAIRS?

JA. MOTHER-IN-LAW IS TOO SICK. SHE NEEDS A GOOD BED.

ANJA'S MOTHER HAD GALLSTONES. THE DAY THE GERMANS CAME SHE LAY IN THE BED.

PLEASE DON'T TAKE HER BED-LOOK AT HOW SICK SHE IS.

THE DOCTOR IS HERE EVERY DAY.

FATHER-IN-LAW HAD AN OLD FRIEND WHO CAME ALWAYS OVER TO PLAY CARDS.

...AND THEY LEFT WITHOUT TAKING ANYTHING!

YOU KNOW, I MET A GERMAN OFFICIAL WHO WOULD PAY WELL FOR A BEDROOM SET...

HIDDEN, WE HAD NO USE FROM THE FURNITURE. SO WE SHLEPPED IT AGAIN UPSTAIRS TO SELL.

YOU HAVE EXCELLENT TASTE IN FURNITURE, HERR ZYLBERBERG. THANK YOU.

MY MEN WILL BE RIGHT BACK TO GET YOUR WIFE'S BED TOO!...

YOU CHEATED US LAST TIME, JEW!

WAIT! I HAVEN'T BEEN PAID, YET.

PLEASE, IF YOU WANT TO STAY ALIVE GO BACK INSIDE.

HE WAS SO UNHAPPY AFTER. SO UNHAPPY!

79

ONE TIME I WAS GOING TO SEE ILZECKI. THIS WAS LATE IN 1941, I THINK. HIS HOUSE WAS VERY NEAR TO A TRAIN STATION...

...AND IT WAS GOING ON THERE SOMETHING TERRIBLE.

I HAD TO PASS NEAR— AND THEY WERE GRABBING JEWS, IF THEY HAD PAPERS OR NO!

WHAT HAD I TO DO?

WILL I WALK SLOWLY, THEY WILL TAKE ME...

WILL I RUN THEY CAN SHOOT ME!

THEN FROM FAR, I SAW ILZECKI WALKING, SO I WENT HASTY OVER TO HIM.

ALLO!

MR. SPIEGELMAN! WHAT ARE YOU DOING HERE? DON'T YOU SEE WHAT'S GOING ON?

QUICK—COME UPSTAIRS WITH ME UNTIL THE TRAINS LEAVE!

ILZECKI LIVED IN A VERY FANCY HOUSE. HE WAS THE ONLY JEW THERE.

SO I SAT WITH HIM AND HIS WIFE A GOOD FEW HOURS. WE HEARD SHOOTING AND SCREAMS.

HE SURVIVED ME MY LIFE THAT TIME.

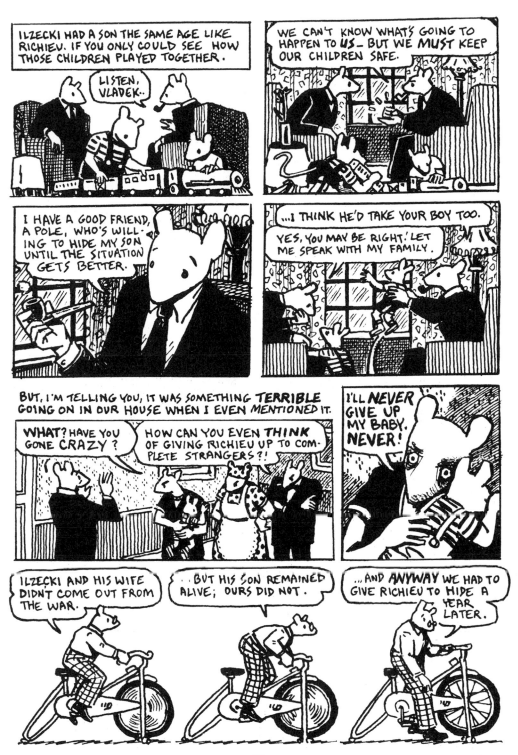

ILZECKI HAD A SON THE SAME AGE LIKE RICHIEU. IF YOU ONLY COULD SEE HOW THOSE CHILDREN PLAYED TOGETHER.

LISTEN, VLADEK..

WE CAN'T KNOW WHAT'S GOING TO HAPPEN TO *US* — BUT WE *MUST* KEEP OUR CHILDREN SAFE.

I HAVE A GOOD FRIEND, A POLE, WHO'S WILLING TO HIDE MY SON UNTIL THE SITUATION GETS BETTER.

...I THINK HE'D TAKE YOUR BOY TOO.

YES, YOU MAY BE RIGHT! LET ME SPEAK WITH MY FAMILY.

BUT, I'M TELLING YOU, IT WAS SOMETHING *TERRIBLE* GOING ON IN OUR HOUSE WHEN I EVEN *MENTIONED* IT.

WHAT? HAVE YOU GONE *CRAZY*?

HOW CAN YOU EVEN *THINK* OF GIVING RICHIEU UP TO COMPLETE STRANGERS?!

I'LL *NEVER* GIVE UP MY BABY. NEVER!

ILZECKI AND HIS WIFE DIDN'T COME OUT FROM THE WAR.

..BUT HIS SON REMAINED ALIVE; OURS DID NOT.

...AND *ANYWAY* WE HAD TO GIVE RICHIEU TO HIDE A YEAR LATER.

81

WHEN WE WERE IN THE GHETTO, IN 1943, TOSHA TOOK ALL THE CHILDREN TO—

WAIT! *PLEASE, DAD. IF YOU DON'T KEEP YOUR STORY CHRON-OLOGICAL, I'LL NEVER GET IT STRAIGHT... TELL ME MORE ABOUT 1941 AND 1942.*

SO?... OKAY. I'LL MAKE IT SO HOW YOU WANT IT. 1941?... AT THE END OF 1941 THE GERMANS CAME WITH SOME-THING NEW. WOLFE RAN FROM THE GEMEINDER...

LOOK! THEY'RE PUTTING THESE UP ALL OVER TOWN.

ORDER

All Jews of Sosnowiec must be relocated into the Stara Sos-nowiec quarter by January 1, 1942. Non-Jews will be moved into vacated premises.

Moneta Merin

ALL 12 OF OUR HOUSEHOLD WERE GIVEN NOW TO LIVE IN 2½ SMALL ROOMS...

REWARD
FOR EVERY UNREGISTERED JEW YOU FIND: 1 KILO of SUGAR

MOST PEOPLE GOT EVEN *LESS* SPACE. BUT FATHER-IN-LAW AND WOLFE HAD A LITTLE *INFLUENCE*...

BUT THIS WASN'T YET A REAL GHETTO. STILL YOU COULD GO INTO OTHER PARTS OF TOWN SO LONG YOU WERE HOME AT NIGHT-TIME

HOLD THE LADDER, ANJA.

I'M PUTTING UP A CURTAIN TO GIVE US SOME PRIVACY.

TOSHA *INSISTED* ON GETTING THE PART OF THE ROOM WITH THE WINDOW.

IT DOESN'T MATTER, VLADEK. I'M JUST GLAD THE WHOLE FAMILY CAN STAY TOGETHER.

IT WAS NO MORE THE LUX-URY LIFE WE HAD BEFORE.

83

BUT WHEN WE CAME TO STARA SOSNOWIEC, ALL MY BUSINESSES BECAME HARDER.... IT WAS NOT SO EASY TO MOVE AROUND.

THE TIN SHOP FINISHED—THE OWNER WAS THE ONLY JEW THEY LET WORK THERE. I GOT THEN A JOB IN A GERMAN CARPENTRY SHOP.

FATHER-IN-LAW AND LOLEK WORKED ALREADY THERE, FOR REALLY NO MONEY. I DIDN'T NEED THIS BEFORE, BUT NOW I HAD TO HAVE THE WORK PAPER.

WOLFE COULD HAVE ARRANGED ME A JOB AT THE GEMEINDE... BUT I DIDN'T WANT TO PUT MY HANDS THERE WHERE JEWS WERE BEING TAKEN.

AND THEN IT CAME *AGAIN* SOMETHING NEW FROM THE GERMANS. WE GOT A NOTICE....

"ALL JEWS OVER 70 YEARS OLD WILL BE TRANSFERED TO THERESIENSTADT IN CZECHOSLOVAKIA ON MAY 10, 1942....

"...A COMMUNITY BETTER PREPARED TO TAKE CARE OF THE ELDERLY THAN OURS IN SOSNOWIEC...."

IT DOESN'T *LOOK* TOO BAD!

LIKE A CONVALESCENT HOME.

NOTICE:

ANJA'S GRANDPARENTS HAD ABOUT 90 YEARS.

WE'VE BEEN TOGETHER —A *FAMILY*—FOR 70 YEARS. WE DON'T WANT TO BREAK APART NOW!

DON'T WORRY. WE WON'T LET THEM TAKE YOU.

WE DIDN'T YET *KNOW* OF AUSCHWITZ—OF THE OVENS—BUT WE WERE ANYWAY AFRAID.

...SO, IN THE YARD, WE MADE A HIDING PLACE, A BUNKER....

CUT-AWAY VIEW:

STORAGE SHEDS

FALSE WALL

GRANDPARENTS

WE SNEAKED FOOD TO THEM, AND-WHEN IT WAS SAFE-WE TOOK THEM INSIDE A LITTLE.

86

SEVERAL TIMES CAME THE JEWISH POLICE TO OUR HOUSE...

OUR RECORDS SHOW THAT MR. AND MRS. KARMIO LIVE HERE. THEY HAVEN'T REGISTERED FOR TRANSFER.

YES- MY WIFE'S PARENTS— THEY LEFT WITHOUT A WORD A MONTH AGO.

JEWISH POLICE?

YES-WITH BIG STICKS.

SOME JEWS THOUGHT IN THIS WAY: IF THEY GAVE TO THE GERMANS A FEW JEWS, THEY COULD SAVE THE REST.

AND AT LEAST THEY COULD SAVE THEMSELVES.

AND A MONTH AFTER, THEY AGAIN CAME TO FATHER-IN-LAW.

MR. ZYLBERBERG, YOU AND YOUR WIFE MUST COME WITH US.

IF THE KARMIOS DON'T TURN UP IN 3 DAYS YOU TWO WILL BE SENT IN THEIR PLACE!

HE HAD STILL A LITTLE "PROTECTION" FROM THE GEMEIN-DE, SO THEY TOOK ONLY HIM AWAY-NOT HIS WIFE.

HE SAT A FEW DAYS THERE, THEN HE SENT TO US A NOTE

HE WROTE THAT WE HAD TO GIVE OVER THE GRANDPARENTS. EVEN IF THEY TOOK ONLY HIM AWAY NOW, NEXT THEY WOULD GRAB HIS WIFE, AND THEN THE REST OF THE FAMILY.

SO, WHAT HAPPENED?

WHAT HAPPENED? WE HAD TO DELIVER THEM!

THEY THOUGHT IT WAS TO THERESIENSTADT THEY WERE GOING.

LET US KNOW IF YOU NEED ANYTHING!

BUT THEY WENT RIGHT AWAY TO AUSCHWITZ, TO THE GAS.

MY FATHER—HE HAD 62 YEARS—CAME BY STREETCAR TO ME FROM DABROWA, THE VILLAGE NEXT DOOR FROM SOSNOWIEC.

AFTER MY MOTHER DIED WITH CANCER, HE LIVED THERE IN THE HOUSE OF MY SISTER FELA, AND HER FOUR SMALL CHILDREN.

HERE'S A COOKIE, RICHIEU. AUNT FELA BAKED IT FOR YOU.

SAY THANK YOU TO GRANDPA.

I NEED YOUR ADVICE, VLADEK. SHOULD I GO TO THE STADIUM ON WEDNESDAY, OR HIDE AT HOME?

I DON'T KNOW. I'M NOT EVEN SURE WHAT WE'RE GOING TO DO. ...ANJA'S MOTHER SAYS SHE ISN'T GOING. SHE'S SICK AND AFRAID.

AT LEAST ANJA'S FATHER, LOLEK AND I ALL WORK AT THE GERMAN WOODSHOP. WE'RE A LITTLE SAFER. BUT YOU DON'T WORK. YOU HAVE NO PAPERS. YOU DON'T HAVE ANYTHING!

WELL, OUR COUSIN MORDECAI SAYS HE'LL BE AT ONE OF THE INSPECTION TABLES. I COULD BRING MY PAPERS TO HIM...

WHAT DOES FELA SAY?

SHE'S NOT SURE...BUT IF FELA DECIDES TO GO, OF COURSE I'LL GO WITH HER.

CAN I HAVE ANOTHER COOKIE?

RICHIEU!

REALLY, I DIDN'T KNOW HOW TO ADVISE HIM.

BUT FINALLY HE DID GO. PEOPLE WERE AFRAID TO NOT SHOW UP.

SO IT CAME TO THE STADIUM ALMOST ALL THE JEWS OF SOSNOWIEC, AND FROM THE OTHER VILLAGES NEAR, MAYBE 25 OR 30,000 PEOPLE.

EVERYONE CAME VERY NICE DRESSED. THEY TRIED SO THAT THEY WOULD LOOK YOUNG AND ABLE TO WORK, IN ORDER TO GET A GOOD STAMP ON THEIR PASSPORT.

WHEN WE WERE EVERYBODY INSIDE, GESTAPO WITH MACHINE GUNS SURROUNDED THE STADIUM.

THEN WAS A SELECTION, WITH PEOPLE SENT EITHER TO THE LEFT, EITHER TO THE RIGHT.

LINE UP BY FAMILY AT THE TABLES TO REGISTER! QUICKLY!

OLD PEOPLE, FAMILIES WITH LOTS OF KIDS, AND PEOPLE WITHOUT WORK CARDS ARE ALL GOING TO THE LEFT!

WE UNDERSTOOD THIS MUST BE VERY BAD.

ME AND ANJA CAME TO THE TABLE WHERE MY COUSIN WAS SITTING...

AH, YOU WORK AT THE CARPENTRY SHOP. GO TO THE RIGHT.

SO WE GOT STAMPED OUR PASSPORTS AND CAME QUICK TO THE GOOD SIDE OF THE STADIUM. THOSE THEY SENT LEFT, THEY DIDN'T GET ANY STAMP.

WE WERE SO HAPPY WE CAME THROUGH. BUT WE WORRIED NOW - WERE OUR FAMILIES SAFE?

LOOK! THERE'S POPPA, WITH LOLEK AND LONIA!

WE SAW WOLFE AND TOSHA. OUR FAMILY SEEMS TO BE OKAY.

DID YOU SEE MY FATHER?

I COULDN'T SEE ANYWHERE MY FATHER.

BUT LATER SOMEONE WHO SAW HIM TOLD ME... HE CAME THROUGH THIS SAME COUSIN OVER TO THE GOOD SIDE.

HER, THEY SENT TO THE LEFT. FOUR CHILDREN WAS TOO MANY.

SPIEGELMAN... TO THE RIGHT.

THEN CAME FELA TO REGISTER...

FELA!

MY DAUGHTER! HOW CAN SHE MANAGE ALONE - WITH FOUR CHILDREN TO TAKE CARE OF?

AND, WHAT DO YOU THINK? HE SNEAKED ON TO THE BAD SIDE!

AND THOSE ON THE BAD SIDE NEVER CAME ANYMORE HOME.

THOSE WITH A STAMP WERE LET TO GO HOME. BUT THERE WERE VERY FEW JEWS NOW LEFT IN SOSNOWIEC...

ONE FROM THREE THEY KEPT AT THE STADIUM.... MAYBE 10,000 PEOPLE - AND WITH THEM, MY FATHER.

WELL....IT'S ENOUGH FOR TODAY. YES, ARTIE?...

91

EVENTUALLY SHE AND MY FATHER BOTH ENDED UP IN AUSCHWITZ. THEY DIED THERE.

WHERE ARE YOU GOING? YOU DIDN'T DRINK YOUR COFFEE.

I JUST THOUGHT OF SOMETHING. MY FATHER MENTIONED THAT ANJA USED TO KEEP A DIARY, AND I *VAGUELY* REMEMBER SEEING THEM ON HIS SHELVES IN THE DEN.

I DOUBT IT. I WOULD HAVE NOTICED THEM.

WELL, THERE'S SO MUCH JUNK IN THERE, IT'S WORTH A SHOT.

LOOK AT ALL THIS STUFF!...OLD MENUS HE PICKED UP ON CRUISES. ...A PILE OF STATIONERY FROM THE PINES HOTEL'...

INCREDIBLE! FOUR 1965 DRY DOCK SAVINGS BANK CALENDARS...I'LL BET HE NEVER EVEN HAD AN ACCOUNT THERE.

HE DRIVES ME CRAZY! HE WON'T EVEN LET ME THROW OUT THE PLASTIC PITCHER HE TOOK FROM HIS HOSPITAL ROOM LAST YEAR!

HE'S MORE ATTACHED TO THINGS THAN TO PEOPLE!

I REALLY DON'T KNOW HOW LONG I CAN TAKE HIM. I REALLY DON'T.

I BETTER BE GETTING HOME. I'LL LOOK FOR THOSE DIARIES NEXT TIME.

WAIT! PUT EVERYTHING BACK EXACTLY LIKE IT WAS, OR I'LL NEVER HEAR THE END OF IT!

OKAY... OKAY... RELAX.

93

THE NEXT WEEK WE SPENT IN MOURNING... MY FATHER'S FRIENDS ALL OFFERED ME HOSTILITY MIXED IN WITH THEIR CONDOLENCES...

ARTHUR—WE'RE SO SORRY...

IT'S HIS FAULT— THE PUNK!

THEY THINK IT'S MY FAULT!!

...BUT, FOR THE MOST PART, I WAS LEFT ALONE WITH MY THOUGHTS...

MENOPAUSAL DEPRESSION
HITLER DID IT!
MOMMY!
BITCH

I REMEMBERED THE LAST TIME I SAW HER...

...ARTIE...

SHE CAME INTO MY ROOM... IT WAS LATE AT NIGHT....

...ARTIE ... YOU ... STILL ... LOVE ... ME .... DON'T YOU? ....

...I TURNED AWAY, RESENTFUL OF THE WAY SHE TIGHTENED THE UMBILICAL CORD...

SURE, MA!

...SHE WALKED OUT AND CLOSED THE DOOR!

CLIK!

AGH!

WELL, MOM, IF YOU'RE LISTENING...

CONGRATULATIONS!... YOU'VE COMMITTED THE PERFECT CRIME ....

...YOU PUT ME HERE .... SHORTED ALL MY CIRCUITS ... CUT MY NERVE ENDINGS ... AND CROSSED MY WIRES!....

...YOU MURDERED ME, MOMMY, AND YOU LEFT ME HERE TO TAKE THE RAP!!!

PIPE DOWN, MAC! SOME OF US ARE TRYING TO SLEEP!

© art spiegelman, 1972

GEE, I'M SURPRISED THAT VLADEK **READ** THIS WHEN HE FOUND IT. HE **NEVER** READS COMICS...

HE DOESN'T EVEN LOOK AT MY WORK WHEN I STICK IT UNDER HIS NOSE.

BUT THIS ISN'T LIKE OTHER COMICS...

I TELL YOU, WHEN RUTHIE SHOWED IT TO ME I THOUGHT I'D **FAINT.** I WAS SO SHOCKED.

IT WAS SO... SO **PERSONAL!**

...BUT VERY ACCURATE... OBJECTIVE. I SPENT A LOT OF TIME HELPING OUT HERE AFTER ANJA'S FUNERAL. IT WAS JUST AS YOU SAID.

SO, ARTIE. I'M READY.

LET'S WALK NOW TO THE BANK TOGETHER.

MALA JUST TOLD ME THAT YOU SAW MY COMIC...THE ONE ABOUT MOM.

YES. I FOUND IT WHEN I LOOKED FOR THE THINGS YOU ASKED ME LAST TIME. **HOO!** I SAW THE PICTURE THERE OF MOM, SO I READ IT... AND I CRIED.

I-I'M SORRY.

IT'S GOOD YOU GOT IT OUTSIDE YOUR SYSTEM. BUT FOR ME IT BROUGHT IN MY MIND SO MUCH **MEMORIES** OF ANJA.

...OF COURSE I'M THINKING ALWAYS ABOUT HER **ANYWAY.**

YES. YOU KEEP PHOTOS OF HER ALL AROUND YOUR DESK—LIKE A SHRINE!

WHAT HAVE I TO DO, MALA? IN THE GARBAGE PUT THEM? OF YOU **ALSO** I HAVE A PHOTO ON THE DESK!

ACH! DON'T DO ME ANY FAVORS!

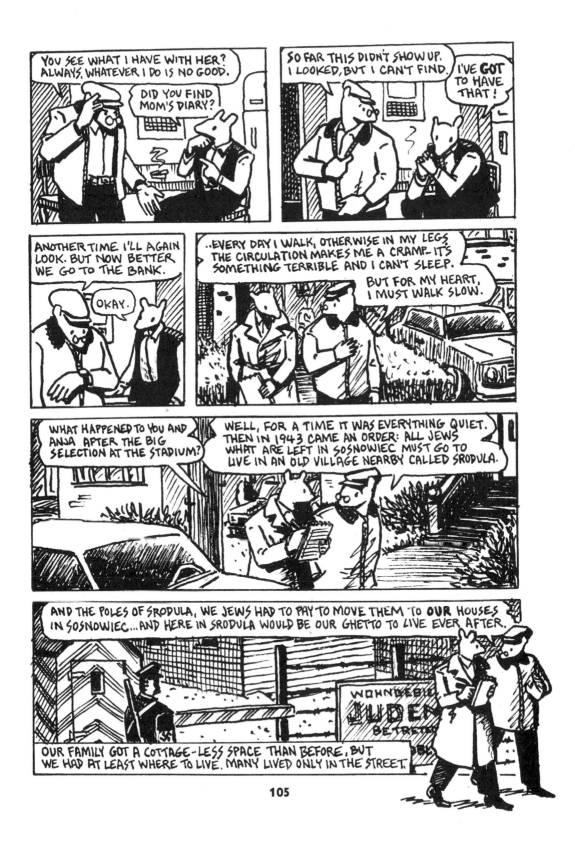

YOU SEE WHAT I HAVE WITH HER? ALWAYS, WHATEVER I DO IS NO GOOD.

DID YOU FIND MOM'S DIARY?

SO FAR THIS DIDN'T SHOW UP. I LOOKED, BUT I CAN'T FIND.

I'VE **GOT** TO HAVE THAT!

ANOTHER TIME I'LL AGAIN LOOK. BUT NOW BETTER WE GO TO THE BANK.

OKAY.

..EVERY DAY I WALK, OTHERWISE IN MY LEGS THE CIRCULATION MAKES ME A CRAMP— IT'S SOMETHING TERRIBLE AND I CAN'T SLEEP.

BUT FOR MY HEART, I MUST WALK SLOW.

WHAT HAPPENED TO YOU AND ANJA AFTER THE BIG SELECTION AT THE STADIUM?

WELL, FOR A TIME IT WAS EVERYTHING QUIET. THEN IN 1943 CAME AN ORDER: ALL JEWS WHAT ARE LEFT IN SOSNOWIEC MUST GO TO LIVE IN AN OLD VILLAGE NEARBY CALLED SRODULA.

AND THE POLES OF SRODULA, WE JEWS HAD TO PAY TO MOVE THEM TO **OUR** HOUSES IN SOSNOWIEC...AND HERE IN SRODULA WOULD BE OUR GHETTO TO LIVE EVER AFTER.

WOHNGEBIE JUDEN BETRE

OUR FAMILY GOT A COTTAGE-LESS SPACE THAN BEFORE, BUT WE HAD AT LEAST WHERE TO LIVE. MANY LIVED ONLY IN THE STREET.

...YOU'VE ALL HEARD THE STORIES ABOUT AUSCHWITZ. HORRIBLE UNBELIEVABLE STORIES.

THEY CAN'T BE TRUE!

ONE THING IS CERTAIN— AS BAD AS THINGS ARE IN THE GHETTO, BEING DEPORTED IS EVEN WORSE.

PLEASE! IT'S BAD LUCK TO EVEN SPEAK OF IT!

LOOK. YOU DON'T HAVE MUCH INFLUENCE HERE. IN ZAWIERCIE I HAVE SOME INFLUENCE WITH THE GERMANS ... I CAN BRIBE THEM.

MY 90-YEAR-OLD FATHER STILL LIVES WITH ME...WHENEVER THERE'S A ROUND-UP, AN S.S. MAN GUARDS HIM TO KEEP HIM SAFE!

NINETY! THIS WAS 1943! IT WASN'T **LEFT** ANY OTHER JEWS WHAT HAD NINETY YEARS!

PERSIS WAS REALLY A FINE MAN—NOT SO LIKE MONIEK MERIN, THE HEAD OF **OUR** GHETTO, WHO LOOKED ONLY OUT FOR HIMSELF. ...PERSIS TRIED REALLY TO HELP HIS JEWS.

I CAN MANAGE PAPERS TO TAKE WOLFE, TOSHA AND BIBI—AND MAYBE LITTLE LONIA AND RICHIEU IF YOU'LL LET ME.

YES. THEY'D BE BETTER OFF.

YOU SEE? I WANTED TO SEND RICHIEU SOMEPLACE SAFE A **YEAR** AGO— WITH ILZECKI'S CHILD!

THINGS ARE EVEN WORSE NOW, VLADEK. WE HAVE NO CHOICE!

NO! WE MUST ALL STAY TOGETHER! WE'VE MADE IT THIS FAR. GOD WILL STILL HELP US!

MATKA! BE REALISTIC!

ANJA'S MOTHER DIDN'T LIKE TO LOOK AT THE FACTS. BUT FINALLY EVEN SHE AGREED,

107

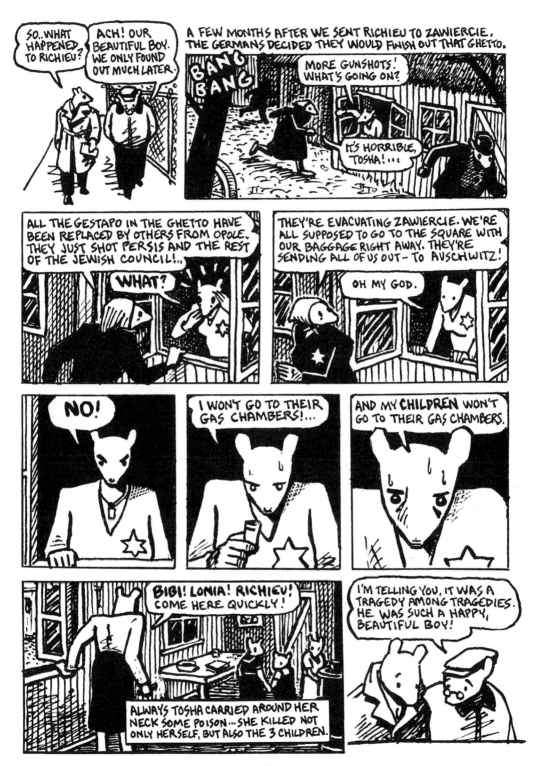

110

111

THEN, IN JUNE, THEY ARRESTED MONIEK MERIN AND ALL THE OTHER HIGHEST BIG SHOTS OF THE *JUDENRAT*, THE JEWISH COUNCIL.

false wall
BUNKER
ATTIC
Entrance hidden by chandelier
UPSTAIRS BEDROOM

AROUND THIS TIME WE WERE PUT INTO A DIFFERENT HOUSE. HERE ALSO WE MADE A BUNKER.

BY THE END OF JULY THE NAZIS MADE TO LIQUIDATE COMPLETELY OUR GHETTO — IT WAS 10,000 JEWS TAKEN AWAY IN ONE WEEK.

EXCEPT TO SNEAK FOR FOOD, WE STAYED MOSTLY IN THE BUNKER.

LOLEK! THANK GOD YOU'RE SAFE!

IT'S LIKE A BATTLEFIELD OUTSIDE!

THERE'S HARDLY ANYONE LEFT IN SRODULA. EVERYONE HAS BEEN DEPORTED OR SHOT.

FROM ALL THE JEWS OF ALL SOSNOWIEC IT WAS LEFT MAYBE 1,000 IN THE GHETTO.

AT LEAST YOUR BAG IS FULL... YOU FOUND A LOT OF FOOD, YES?

JUST A FEW OLD TURNIPS... AND SOME BOOKS.

BOOKS!? WHAT'S THE MATTER WITH YOU? WE CAN'T EAT BOOKS!

SHH

ALL THE TIME WE WERE HUNGRY. WE JUST DIDN'T HAVE WHAT TO EAT.

112

ONE NIGHT WE WENT TO SNEAK FOR FOOD...

LOOK! A STRANGER!

WE DRAGGED HIM UP TO OUR BUNKER

WHAT ARE YOU DOING HERE?

I-I DIDN'T KNOW ANYONE LIVED HERE! I JUST STOPPED TO REST A MOMENT.

MY WIFE AND I HAVE A STARVING BABY. I WAS OUT HUNTING FOR SCRAPS!

HE'S LYING!

IN THE MORNING WE GAVE A LITTLE FOOD TO HIM AND LEFT HIM GO TO HIS FAMILY...

JUDEN RAUS!

HE MAY BE AN INFORMER. THE SAFEST THING WOULD BE TO KILL HIM!

WHAT HAD WE TO DO? WE TOOK ON HIM PITY.

...THE GESTAPO CAME THAT AFTERNOON.

THEY TOOK US TO A BUILDING IN A PART OF SRODULA SEPARATED BY WIRES— A GHETTO INSIDE THE GHETTO—AND THERE WE HAD TO SIT AND TO WAIT.

118

I TOLD HASKEL AND MILOCH LATER ABOUT THIS.

YOU WERE VERY LUCKY, VLADEK...

THEY CALL HIM "THE SHOOTER". EVERY DAY HE KILLS SOME POOR JEW, JUST FOR FUN.

HEY! AREN'T YOU GOING OVER TO PESACH'S TO BUY SOME CAKE?

CAKE?

FOR YEARS WE DIDN'T SEE ANY CAKE. HARDLY EVEN **BREAD** WE SAW!

IT'S IMPOSSIBLE!

HE'S JOKING!

CAKE!

BUT COUSIN PESACH WAS REALLY SELLING **CAKE**! EVERYONE WHAT COULD AFFORD IT STOOD ON LINE TO BUY A PIECE...

IT LOOKS DELICIOUS.

HOW DID YOU MANAGE IT, PESACH?

WHEN PEOPLE ARE SENT TO AUSCHWITZ, MY MEN SEARCH THEIR HOUSES.

PESACH WAS LIKE HASKEL, PART OF THE JEWISH POLICE.

THEY FIND A LITTLE FLOUR HERE, A FEW GRAMS OF SUGAR THERE...I SAVED IT!

HE WAS YOUNGER FROM HASKEL, BUT ALSO A "KOMBINATOR."

YOU KNOW WHAT A COOK MY RIFKA IS...TRY IT! ONLY 75 ZLOTYS A SLICE.

I HAD STILL SAVINGS, SO I GOT FOR ANJA AND ME SOME CAKE.

BUT, THE WHOLE GHETTO, WE WERE SO SICK LATER, YOU CAN'T IMAGINE...

SOME OF THE FLOUR PESACH FOUND—IT WASN'T *REALLY* FLOUR, ONLY **LAUNDRY SOAP**, WHAT HE PUT IN THE CAKE BY MISTAKE.

OW! * GROAN OY! * OUCH!

...WE WERE, ALL OF US, SICK LIKE DOGS.

BEFORE THE WAR, PESACH HAD A RESORT HOTEL IN ZAKOPANE...
IN THOSE DAYS ALSO HE FOUND ALWAYS SCHEMES.

ALL GUESTS HAD TO PAY BIG POLISH TAXES... SO PESACH TOOK BRIBES TO NOT REGISTER THEM. BUT IF AN INSPECTOR CAME, THE GUESTS HAD TO HIDE THEMSELVES AWAY.

ONE TIME HIS WIFE MADE NOT ENOUGH DESSERTS TO GIVE TO EVERYBODY... SO PESACH RAN INTO THE DINING ROOM AND YELLED, "INSPECTORS ARE COMING!"

IT WAS NO INSPECTOR, OF COURSE. BUT 40% OF THE GUESTS RAN FAST FROM THE ROOM. ...PESACH HAD ENOUGH DESSERTS LEFT OVER EVEN FOR THE NEXT DAY!
COME.

ARE YOU READY TO WALK AGAIN?

YES, IT'S TOO DIRTY TO SIT! ...BUT, REALLY, IF I DIDN'T HAVE MY NITROSTAT, IT COULD HAVE BEEN JUST NOW SOMETHING TERRIBLE.

MILOCH SPIEGELMAN—HE SURVIVED THE WAR WITH HIS WIFE AND CHILD AND THEY MOVED TO AUSTRALIA. ABOUT FIVE YEARS AGO HE GOT A BIG HEART ATTACK...

AND LAST YEAR, HE GOT ON THE STREET A SEIZURE—LIKE WHAT I HAD JUST NOW... BUT HE DIDN'T HAVE WITH HIM HIS PILLS. HIS WIFE RAN TO FIND A DRUG STORE.
WHEN SHE CAME BACK MILOCH WAS DEAD!

NU? SO LIFE GOES. BUT I MUST FINISH QUICK TO TELL YOU THE REST ABOUT SRODULA, BECAUSE WE WILL COME SOON OVER TO THE BANK.

SALE

120

BY THE END OF 1943 THE VANS WENT EVERY WEDNESDAY WITH MORE AND MORE AND MORE PEOPLE FROM SRODULA TO AUSCHWITZ UNTIL IT WAS VERY FEW LEFT.

IT COULD BE OUR TURN SOON, EH VLADEK?

LET'S HOPE NOT, MILOCH.

HASKEL HEARD THAT ANY DAY NOW THEY INTEND TO DEPORT EVERYONE THAT'S STILL LEFT HERE.

MILOCH TOOK ME TO THE SHOE SHOP

IT WAS EARLY AND NOBODY WAS THERE...

HASKEL MADE PLANS TO SMUGGLE HIMSELF OUT OF THE GHETTO.

PESACH AND I HAVE A PLAN ALSO...

HE MOVED A FEW SHOES FROM A PILE HIGH TO THE CEILING...

...AND TOOK ME INSIDE A TUNNEL...

DON'T TELL ANYONE ABOUT THIS EXCEPT ANJA AND YOUR NEPHEW.

...A TUNNEL MADE FROM SHOES!

WE CAME OUT TO A BUNKER...

BE PREPARED TO BRING THEM ON A MOMENT'S NOTICE!

INCREDIBLE!

EVERYTHING WAS READY HERE SO 15 OR 16 PEOPLE COULD HIDE.

...BUT WHEN ANJA AND I APPROACHED TO DISCUSS THIS BUNKER WITH LOLEK...

NO THANKS, FORGET IT!

BUT MILOCH ORGANIZED EVERYTHING!

I'M SICK OF HIDING!

OUR NEPHEW WAS THEN ONLY 15. HE WAS WORKING AS AN ELECTRICIAN.

ALWAYS LOLEK WAS A LITTLE MESHUGA...

I'M A SKILLED WORKER. WHEREVER THEY TAKE ME, I'LL BE OKAY.

YOU'RE CRAZY! YOU'RE GOING STRAIGHT TO THE OVENS!

AND HE DID GET PUT INTO ONE OF THE NEXT TRANSPORTS TO AUSCHWITZ.

ANJA BECAME COMPLETELY HYSTERICAL.

THE WHOLE FAMILY IS GONE! GRANDMA AND GRANDPA! POPPA! MOMMA! TOSHA! BIBI! MY RICHIEU!!

NOW THEY'LL TAKE LOLEK!

IT WAS ALSO AROUND THIS TIME THAT WE HEARD FIRST THE BAD NEWS FROM ZAWIERCIE-ABOUT TOSHA AND RICHIEU.

OH GOD. LET ME DIE TOO!

COME, ANJA. GET UP!

WHY ARE YOU PULLING ME, VLADEK? LET ME ALONE! I DON'T WANT TO LIVE!

NO, DARLING! TO DIE, IT'S EASY...

BUT YOU HAVE TO STRUGGLE FOR LIFE!

UNTIL THE LAST MOMENT WE MUST STRUGGLE TOGETHER! I NEED YOU!

AND YOU'LL SEE THAT TOGETHER WE'LL SURVIVE.

THIS ALWAYS I TOLD TO HER.

THE GHETTO FINISHED OUT SO LIKE MILOCH SAID. ABOUT TWELVE FROM US RAN INTO HIS BUNKER WITH HIM, HIS WIFE AND HIS THREE-YEARS-OLD BABY BOY.

GUTCHA, YOU'VE GOT TO KEEP THE BABY QUIET!

HUSH.

WAAH! I'M HUNGRY!

WE'LL HAVE TO KEEP HIM UNDER BLANKETS UNTIL HE CALMS DOWN.

IN A BUNKER IN ANOTHER PART FROM THE SHOE SHOP LAY PESACH AND SOME OTHERS.

IT WAS NOTHING TO DO ALL DAY BUT TO LIE AND TO STARVE.

THE WHOLE DAY AND NIGHT ANJA SAT WRITING INTO HER NOTEBOOK.

THERE! I'VE MANAGED TO DIG A SMALL HOLE IN THE STONE WALL.

I CAN SEE SOLDIERS.

ALL AROUND WERE GUARDS TO FIND ANY WHO REMAINED HIDING.

WHAT LITTLE FOOD WE HAD, SOON IT WAS GONE.

OHH... I WISH I HAD SOME BREAD... I WISH I HAD SOME BREAD... I WISH—

QUIET! WE'RE ALL STARVING!

AT NIGHT WE SNEAKED OUT TO LOOK FOR WHAT TO EAT... BUT IT WAS NOTHING TO FIND.

HERE, ANJA— CHEW ON THIS.

YOU FOUND FOOD?

NEVER, ANY OF US HAD BEEN SO HUNGRY LIKE THEN.

NO, IT'S ONLY WOOD. BUT CHEWING IT FEELS A LITTLE LIKE EATING FOOD.

123

AFTER A TIME PESACH CAME OVER TO US FROM HIS BUNKER....

MAYBE YOU FOOLS ARE WILLING TO LIE HERE UNTIL YOU STARVE TO DEATH—BUT NOT ME!...

I'VE CONTACTED ONE OF THE GUARDS.

IT'LL COST A FORTUNE, BUT HE'S AGREED TO LOOK THE OTHER WAY.

OUR GROUP WILL MIX IN WITH THE POLES WHEN THEY WALK PAST SRODULA ON THE WAY TO WORK TOMORROW... IF YOU WANT TO CHIP IN YOU CAN COME WITH US.

MANY FROM OUR BUNKER SAID YES.

MILOCH AND I, WE SAID NO TO THIS IDEA. WE DIDN'T TRUST TO THE GERMANS.

ONE GUY FROM OUR BUNKER, AVRAM, CAME TO ME.

HE SAID, "TELL ME WHEN *YOU* WILL GO OUT, VLADEK. *THEN* I'LL KNOW IT'S SAFE."

HE AND HIS GIRLFRIEND WANTED TO PAY ME TO ADVISE.

THEY HAD STILL 2 WATCHES AND SOME DIAMOND RINGS. I DIDN'T WANT TO TAKE. THEY *NEEDED* THESE TO LIVE.

SO I TOOK ONLY THE SMALL WATCH.

BANK

THE NEXT MORNING, VERY EARLY, THE GROUP WALKED OUT.

THEY GAVE OVER THE MONEY AND WENT PAST THE GUARD.

TAKKA TAKKA TAK

I STOOD, SECRET, BEHIND A CORNER. I HEARD LOUD SHOOTING, AND I DIDN'T GO TO SEE WHAT HAPPENED...

I ONLY RAN VERY FAST BACK TO OUR BUNKER.

ONLY A FEW OF US REMAINED.

THERE HAVEN'T BEEN ANY LIGHTS ON IN THE GUARD-HOUSE FOR TWO NIGHTS... I THINK IT'S SAFE.

A LITTLE BEFORE DAWN WE WENT OUT FROM SRODULA...

THEY'RE ALL GONE!

WHEW

THE GHETTO IS EMPTY!

AHEAD OF TIME WE ORGANIZED OUR-SELVES GOOD CLOTHES AND I.D. PAPERS.

WE MIXED WITH THE POLES GOING TO WORK.

WE'LL BE HIDING AT THIS AD-DRESS. WHEN YOU FIND A SAFE PLACE, TRY TO CONTACT US, VLADEK.

GOOD LUCK, MILOCH.

WE WENT ALL IN DIF-FERENT DIRECTIONS.

THAT GUY, AVRAM, HIS WOMAN HAD FRIENDS TO KEEP THEM.

AND THE FRIENDS KEPT THEM... UNTIL AVRAM'S MONEY FINISHED. THEN THEY WERE REPORTED.

ANJA AND I DIDN'T HAVE WHERE TO GO.

WE WALKED IN THE DIRECTION OF SOSNOWIEC – BUT *WHERE TO GO?!*

IT WAS *NOWHERE* WE HAD TO HIDE.

CAN I HELP YOU, MR. SPIEGELMAN?

YES, I HAVE HERE MY SON, ARTIE. I WANT TO SIGN HIM A KEY. SO HE CAN GO ALSO TO MY SAFETY BOX.

127

Another visit...

ANYBODY HOME? THE DOOR WASN'T LOCKED, SO I ...

HUH? MALA? WERE YOU CRYING?

NO. SNK I DON'T KNOW. I TELL YOU, I'M AT MY WITS' END!

WHAT NOW?

YOUR FATHER! HE TREATS ME AS IF I WERE JUST A MAID OR HIS NURSE... **WORSE!**

AT LEAST A MAID HAS SOME DAYS OFF AND GETS PAID!

HE ONLY GIVES ME $50.00 A MONTH. WHEN I NEED A PAIR OF STOCKINGS I HAVE TO USE MY OWN SAVINGS!

WELL... HE HASN'T CHANGED...

WHENEVER I NEEDED SCHOOL SUPPLIES OR NEW CLOTHES MOM WOULD HAVE TO PLEAD AND ARGUE FOR **WEEKS** BEFORE HE'D COUGH UP ANY DOUGH!

WHEN **I** TRY TO ARGUE WITH HIM HE MOANS LIKE HE'S GOING TO HAVE ANOTHER HEART ATTACK.

I CAN'T BE SURE IF HE'S FAKING, SO I HAVE TO STOP!

I FEEL LIKE I'M IN PRISON!

I FEEL LIKE I'M GOING TO **BURST!**

135

136

139

140

AT THE BLACK MARKET I SAW SEVERAL TIMES A NICE WOMAN, WHAT I MADE A LITTLE FRIENDS WITH HER...

GOOD MORNING, MR. SPIEGELMAN.

HOW DO YOU DO, MRS. MOTONOWA! WHAT DO YOU HAVE IN YOUR BASKET TODAY?

HOW ABOUT A LOAF OF FRESH BREAD?

FINE, FINE.

OH. I'M SORRY. I DON'T HAVE ANY CHANGE.

IT'S OKAY... KEEP IT FOR YOUR LITTLE BOY.

ARE YOU AND YOUR WIFE STILL LIVING IN A BARN?

WE HAVEN'T FOUND ANYTHING BETTER.

I'VE BEEN THINKING ABOUT IT... WHY DON'T YOU BOTH MOVE IN WITH MY SON AND ME?

WHAT ABOUT YOUR HUSBAND?

HE WORKS IN GERMANY, AND ONLY COMES HOME FOR 10 DAYS EVERY 3 MONTHS... I'LL KEEP YOU HIDDEN IN THE CELLAR WHEN HE'S AROUND.

IT SOUNDS GOOD TO ME, BUT IT'S OVER 20 KILOMETERS TO YOUR HOUSE IN SZOPIENICE. MY WIFE WILL BE AFRAID TO GO!

DON'T WORRY. I'LL ESCORT YOU!

THE NEXT EVENING SHE CAME WITH HER 7-YEARS-OLD BOY TO KAWKA'S FARMHOUSE...

I WALKED WITH MOTONOWA AS IF *SHE* WAS MY WIFE.

AND ANJA, LIKE A GOVERNESS, WENT WITH THE LITTLE BOY BEHIND. AND NOBODY EVEN *LOOKED* ON US.

WE HAD HERE A LITTLE COMFORTABLE ... WE HAD WHERE TO SIT.

REMEMBER, LITTLE ONE — NEVER TELL ANYBODY THERE ARE JEWS HERE. THEY'LL SHOOT US ALL!

YES, AUNT ANJA.

THE LITTLE BOY WAS VERY SMART AND HE LOVED VERY MUCH ANJA.

YOU HAD TO PAY MRS. MOTONOWA TO KEEP YOU, RIGHT?

OF COURSE I PAID ... AND WELL I PAID.

... WHAT YOU THINK? SOMEONE WILL RISK THEIR LIFE FOR NOTHING?

... I PAID ALSO FOR THE FOOD WHAT SHE GAVE TO US FROM HER SMUGGLING BUSINESS.

BUT, ONE TIME I MISSED A FEW COINS TO THE BREAD ...

I'LL PAY YOU THE REST TOMORROW, AFTER I GO OUT AND CASH SOME VALUABLES.

SORRY ... I WASN'T ABLE TO FIND ANY BREAD TODAY.

ALWAYS SHE GOT BREAD, SO I DIDN'T BELIEVE ... BUT, STILL, SHE WAS A GOOD WOMAN.

IN HIS SCHOOL THE BOY WAS VERY BAD IN GERMAN. SO ANJA TUTORED TO HIM.

ICH BIN ... DU BIST ... ER IST ...

SHE KNEW GERMAN LIKE AN EXPERT.

AND SOON HE CAME OUT WITH VERY GOOD GRADES.

MY TEACHER ASKED ME HOW I IMPROVED SO MUCH ...

SO I TOLD HIM MY MOTHER WAS HELPING ME.

WHEW

HE WAS REALLY A CLEVER BOY.

142

143

144

BUT, THEN, MOTONOWA STOPPED TO COME DOWN.

IT'S BEEN 3 DAYS SINCE SHE BROUGHT ANY FOOD.

HERE... HAVE AN-OTHER CANDY...

I HAD STILL CANDIES I ORGANIZED ON DEKERTA. ONLY **THIS** WE HAD TO EAT.

ALSO, HERE WE HAD NO PLACE WHERE TO WASH, SO ANJA GOT ON ALL HER SKIN A TERRIBLE RASH.

I DON'T KNOW WHAT'S WORSE—THE HUNGER OR THE ITCHING.

DON'T SCRATCH! IT ONLY— SHH!

KLIK

THE DOOR.

I'M SORRY I COULDN'T GET DOWN BEFORE... MY HUSBAND IS GETTING SUSPICIOUS.

HE ASKED WHY I GO TO THE CELLAR SO OFTEN. HE EVEN ASKED IF I WAS HIDING **JEWS** HERE! ...HE WAS **JOKING**, BUT STILL...

ARE YOU ALL RIGHT HERE?

THERE ARE **RATS**, GIANT RATS! THEY'RE HORRIBLE!

WELL— YOU'RE BETTER OFF WITH THE RATS THAN WITH THE GESTAPO... AT LEAST THE RATS WON'T **KILL** YOU!

MMM..

AND SHE WAS RIGHT. WE WERE HAPPY EVEN TO HAVE **THESE** CONDITIONS.

AFTER THE TEN DAYS HER HUSBAND LEFT, AND SHE TOOK US BACK.

IT'S GOOD TO BE "HOME," EH, VLADEK?

IT'S A LOT NICER THAN THAT CELLAR.

BUT I DIDN'T FEEL SAFE HERE. IT WAS TOO MANY WAYS SOME-BODY COULD FIND US OUT. I WANT-ED TO GO BETTER TO HUNGARY.

WHEN I ARRIVED TO KAWKA, THE TWO SMUGGLERS WERE THERE TOGETHER SITTING IN THE KITCHEN..

PLEASE WAIT IN THE OTHER ROOM. THEY'LL SEE YOU SOON.

MR. MANDELBAUM!

VLADEK SPIEGELMAN!

MANDELBAUM, BEFORE THE WAR OWNED A SWEETS SHOP.

ANJA AND I BOUGHT ALWAYS PASTRIES THERE. HE USED TO BE A VERY RICH MAN IN SOSNOWIEC.

THIS IS MY WIFE...AND YOU KNOW MY NEPHEW..

HELLO, ABRAHAM. WHAT ARE YOU ALL DOING HERE?

BACK WHEN IT WAS THE GHETTO, ABRAHAM WAS A BIG MEMBER OF THE JEWISH COUNCIL.

WE'RE TRYING TO GET OUT OF POLAND—

—TO HUNGARY?! YES. ANJA AND I ARE TRYING TO ARRANGE THAT TOO!

THE SMUGGLERS PROPOSED US HOW THEY WOULD DO.

...AND AT THE BORDER OUR PARTNERS WILL TAKE YOU THROUGH THE MOUNTAINS.

WHEW— IT'S RISKY AND VERY EXPENSIVE!

WE SPOKE YIDDISH SO THE POLES DON'T UNDERSTAND.

NIE, VAS DENKST DIE?

YECH KENN DIE FRAU KAWKA, UBER YECH BIN NISH ZICHER VEGEN DIE ZWEI.

So, what do you think?

I know Mrs. Kawka, but I'm not sure about these two.

HERR MECHTSE! YECH GEI KOIDEM MIT ZEI. AZ ALLES VET ZEIN BESEDER, YECH VIL SCHREIBEN TSE DEYER.

Listen! I'll go first. If everything is okay, I'll write back to you.

THE OTHERS WANT TO THINK ABOUT IT A LITTLE LONGER, BUT I'M READY TO GO NOW.

FINE, FINE.

I AGREED WITH MANDELBAUM TO MEET AGAIN HERE. IF IT CAME A GOOD LETTER, WE'LL GO.

150

THE JANITOR IN THE HOUSE MILOCH OWNED, SHE HID NOW HIM AND HIS FAMILY; BUT -OH BOY- HE WAS IN A SITUATION WORSE AS I COULD IMAGINE!

I WENT TO THE JANITOR BY TROLLEY

HELLO- I'M MILOCH'S COUSIN, VLADEK.

YES. HE TOLD ME YOU MIGHT COME.

I HAVE SOME COMPANY UPSTAIRS. I CAN'T TAKE YOU TO MILOCH UNTIL THEY LEAVE.

GENTLEMEN. THIS IS MY COUSIN, VLADEK.

HI "CUZ," HAVE A DRINK.

SO WE TALKED, AND THEY BELIEVED I AM *HER* COUSIN.

WE'RE ALMOST OUT OF VODKA. BRING SOME MORE, MEINKA.

THERE ISN'T ANY.

BAH! SHE'S HIDING HER VODKA!

JUST LIKE SHE'S HIDING JEWS IN HER YARD!

THE JANITOR AND I FROZE OUR BLOOD FROM FEAR...

IF YOU DON'T PUT ANOTHER BOTTLE ON THE TABLE *RIGHT AWAY*, WE'LL TELL THE GESTAPO ABOUT THE JEWS YOU'RE KEEPING!!

R-RELAX FELLOWS.

HERE'S A FEW MARKS, MEINKA. RUN DOWNSTAIRS AND GET ANOTHER BOTTLE FOR OUR FRIENDS.

'ATTA BOY. HIC.

IN 15 MINUTES SHE CAME WITH A BOTTLE AND THEY WERE HAPPY.

YOU SEE? YOUR COUSIN KNOWS HOW TO ENTERTAIN GUESTS! TO YOUR HEALTH.

WE DRANK AND WE DRANK- ONLY NEAR MIDNIGHT FINALLY THEY WENT HOME.

I THINK IT'S SAFE TO GO DOWN.

ARE YOU -SNF- CARRYING *FOOD* FOR MILOCH?

I FED THEM EARLIER. THIS IS JUST *TRASH*.

THE CONDITIONS HOW MILOCH WAS LIVING-YOU COULDN'T BELIEVE.

...I ALWAYS BRING GARBAGE SO THE NEIGHBORS DON'T GET SUSPICIOUS.

PSST-MILOCH. YOUR COUSIN IS HERE.

?

IN EACH COURTYARD WAS A VERY DEEP HOLE TO THROW IN ALL THE GARBAGE.

INSIDE THIS GARBAGE HOLE WAS HERE SEPARATED A TINY SPACE — MAYBE ONLY 5 FEET BY 6 FEET.

VLADEK! I'M GLAD YOU'RE STILL ALIVE!

MY GOD!

I LOOKED DOWN ONLY FOR A SECOND, BUT IN THERE WAS LIVING MILOCH, HIS WIFE AND THEIR 3-YEARS-OLD BOY.

HOW CAN YOU *LIVE* THERE? YOU MUST BE FREEZING!

WE HAVE NO CHOICE. AT LEAST OUR BUNKER IS UNDERGROUND...

AND THE DECOMPOSING GARBAGE GIVES SOME HEAT.

BUT PEOPLE *KNOW* YOU'RE IN THERE...

I TOLD HIM MY STORY WITH THESE POLES UPSTAIRS.

WHAT CAN WE DO?

LISTEN-ANJA AND I MAY BE GOING TO HUNGARY!..

I EXPLAINED OUR HIDING PLACE WAS NOT PERFECT, BUT BETTER THAN HIS.

I'LL COME AGAIN WHEN I HAVE MORE NEWS, BUT IT'S VERY LATE NOW — I MUST GET BACK HOME.

AND I WAS LUCKY. NOBODY MADE ME ANY QUESTIONS GOING BACK TO SZOPIENICE.

153

154

I HAD A SMALL BAG TO TRAVEL. WHEN THEY REGISTERED ME IN, THEY LOOKED OVER EVERYTHING.

WHAT'S THIS? SHOE POLISH??

YES. I LIKE TO KEEP MYSELF NEAT.

WITH A SPOON HE TOOK OUT, LITTLE BY LITTLE, ALL THE POLISH.

WELL, WELL...A GOLD WATCH. YOU JEWS ALWAYS HAVE GOLD!

WRAPPED IN FOIL, I KEPT IT HIDDEN THERE... IT WAS MY LAST TREASURE.

IT WAS THIS WATCH I GOT FROM FATHER-IN-LAW WHEN FIRST I MARRIED TO ANJA.

WELL, NEVER MIND...THEY TOOK IT AND THREW ME WITH MANDELBAUM INTO A CELL...

WAIT A MINUTE! WHAT EVER HAPPENED TO ABRAHAM?

WHO?

-BUT

AH, MANDELBAUM'S NEPHEW! YES. HE FINISHED THE SAME AS US TO CONCENTRATION CAMP.

YES. I'LL TELL YOU HOW IT WAS WITH HIM - BUT NOW I'M TELLING HERE IN THE PRISON...

HERE WE GOT VERY LITTLE TO EAT—MAYBE SOUP ONE TIME A DAY—AND WE SAT WITH NOTHING TO DO.

WHY DON'T THEY PUT US TO WORK LIKE THE REST OF YOU?

IT MEANS YOU WON'T BE HERE VERY LONG...

...EVERY WEEK OR SO A TRUCK TAKES SOME OF THE PRISONERS AWAY.

EXCUSE ME... DO ANY OF YOU KNOW GERMAN?

MY FAMILY JUST SENT ME A FOOD PARCEL. IF I WRITE BACK THEY'LL SEND ANOTHER, BUT WE'RE ONLY ALLOWED TO WRITE GERMAN.

I KNEW WELL TO WRITE GERMAN...SO I WROTE...

IN A SHORT TIME HE GOT AGAIN A PACKAGE...

YOU DID A GREAT JOB! TAKE ANYTHING YOU WANT FOR YOU AND YOUR FRIEND!

IT WAS EGGS THERE...IT WAS EVEN CHOCOLATES. ...I WAS VERY LUCKY TO GET SUCH GOODIES!

158

AFTER ANJA DIED I HAD TO MAKE AN ORDER WITH EVERYTHING... THESE PAPERS HAD TOO MANY MEMORIES. SO I **BURNED** THEM.

YOU **BURNED** THEM?

CHRIST! YOU SAVE **TONS** OF WORTHLESS SHIT, AND YOU...,

YES, IT'S A SHAME! FOR **YEARS** THEY WERE LAYING THERE AND NOBODY EVEN LOOKED IN.

DID YOU EVER **READ** ANY OF THEM? ... CAN YOU REMEMBER WHAT SHE WROTE?

NO. I LOOKED IN, BUT I DON'T REMEMBER...ONLY I KNOW THAT SHE SAID, "I WISH MY SON, WHEN HE GROWS UP, HE WILL BE INTERESTED BY THIS."

GOD **DAMN** YOU! YOU-YOU **MURDERER!** HOW THE HELL COULD YOU **DO** SUCH A THING!!

ACH

TO YOUR **FATHER** YOU YELL IN THIS WAY? ... EVEN TO YOUR **FRIENDS** YOU SHOULD NEVER YELL THIS WAY!

BUT, I'M TELLING YOU, AFTER THE TRAGEDY WITH MOTHER, I WAS SO **DEPRESSED** THEN, I DIDN'T KNOW IF I'M COMING OR I'M GOING!

I'M SORRY. LOOK, POP. IT'S GETTING LATE. I'D BETTER GET HOME...

COME. FIRST UP-STAIRS FOR A LITTLE COFFEE.

NO...REALLY. I'D BETTER GET GOING RIGHT AWAY...

SO,...TELEPHONE TO ME... YOU SHOULD VISIT HERE MORE OFTEN...DON'T BE SUCH A **STRANGER!**

SURE... YOU BET! SO LONG.

...MURDERER.

 159

NOW AVAILABLE:

Maus: A Survivor's Tale

Part II: And Here My Troubles Began

(From Mauschwitz to the Catskills and Beyond)